Northamptonshire's Lost Railways

by
David Blagrove

In all the glory of its shiny black paint, an LNWR Webb 0-6-0 bustles into Oundle Station on the Nene Valley line with a train from Northampton some time during the Edwardian period. Oundle Station was a particularly fine example of how the railway company interpreted the local architectural vernacular, and demonstrates the typical Northamptonshire features of mullioned windows, parapeted gables and kneeler stones. The station was sited on the far bank of the River Nene from the town it served, connection being made by means of an ancient bridge. In this view the approaching train appears to be on the wrong line, but it is in fact on the right one. The down platform was sited some yards north of the up platform. The train appears to be about to negotiate that most archaic piece of railway equipment, a wagon turntable. This device enabled a short wheelbase wagon to be detached from the middle of a train and run off at right angles. It was a great saver of space, saved shunting movements and was extremely useful in a cramped location such as Oundle. However, HM Railway Inspectorate eventually set its face against such practices in the interests of safety.

First published in the United Kingdom, 2003,
Republished 2007, 2010,
by Stenlake Publishing Ltd,
01290 551122
www.stenlake.co.uk

ISBN 9781840332513

ACKNOWLEDGEMENTS

The publishers wish to thank the following for contributing photographs to this book: John Alsop for the front cover and pages 1, 2, 5, 6, 8, 12, 13, 16, 23–26, 28, 30, 32, 35, 36, 40–42, and 45–47; and Richard Casserley for the inside front cover and pages 4, 7, 9–11, 14, 15, 17–22, 27, 29, 31, 33, 34, 37–39, 43, 44, 48, the inside back cover and the back cover.

A GCR express at speed near Brackley in the early days of the GCR London Extension, behind Robinson 4-4-0 No. 1040. Note the carriages finished in brown and cream; this livery was changed to teak in 1910.

INTRODUCTION

Northamptonshire and its one-time appendage, The Soke of Peterborough, is one of Britain's most inland counties, and is still one of the most rural in southern England. It extends from Fenland to the Cherwell Valley on the edge of the Cotswolds and consequently lies across the axis of routes from London to the north and midlands. This has resulted in a complex of communications across the county, ranging from pre-Roman tracks to the latest fibre-optic networks. The county's railway history reflects this.

The very first iron railway in the south of England was laid between Stoke Bruerne and Blisworth during the construction of the Grand Junction Canal in 1800. It was a plateway, worked by horses, and enabled the canal company to open as a through route before the completion of Blisworth tunnel. Other railways were laid in connection with canal construction at Cosgrove and Crick, and from 1805 until 1815 a similar plateway connected the main canal at Gayton Junction with Northampton. All these lines became redundant as the canal system expanded or was completed.

Fifteen years after the Northampton plateway was replaced by the Northampton arm of the Grand Junction Canal, Robert Stephenson, then aged 27, received a commission for a survey for a railway from London to Birmingham. After a colossal Parliamentary battle an Act was passed in May 1833. Construction of the line took five years, including two major constructions in Northamptonshire at Roade cutting and Kilsby tunnel. Almost as soon as the London & Birmingham (L&BR) was completed other railways sought to join it for a route to London, overloading its line with traffic. Rival routes also materialised, and the prospect of the broad gauge Great Western Railway (GWR) making a junction at Rugby and thus acquiring running powers to the north frightened the L&BR shareholders into merging with their fellow companies on the west side of the country to form the London & North Western Railway (LNWR) in 1846.

The LNWR was determined to keep the GWR out of its western flanks and so supported the construction of cross-country lines towards Oxford and Banbury. Similarly it promoted lines on its eastern side with a similar view to keeping other companies away from its territory. The L&BR had promoted a long branch down the Nene Valley to Peterborough and its successor pushed through lines from Northampton to Market Harborough and from Rugby to Peterborough along the northern borders of the county. None of these lines passed through areas of industrial importance, but during the 'Mania Years' of the 1840s various rival mainline schemes were proposed which would intersect them. Of these the Midland Railway extension south from Leicester and the Great Northern Railway (GNR) from London to Doncaster came to fruition in the 1850s.

The Midland's extension was the scheme which had the most profound influence upon Northamptonshire's industry, for it both stimulated the shoe industry of Kettering and the central part of the county and helped the expansion of the burgeoning iron industry. Eventually both the Midland and the LNWR came to share in this increased prosperity. Peterborough boomed with its increased importance to the rail network, and improved railways assisted the growth of the brick industry while Northampton's shoemakers were forced to mechanise in order to keep up with their competitors served by the Midland. Over the next decades the county town and the cathedral city expanded, but the population in rural areas stagnated, or even fell.

A boom in the iron industry during the early 1860s resulted in the promotion of lines from east to west across Northamptonshire in the hope of drawing lucrative traffic to the furnaces of south Wales. Of these schemes the only ones that came to fruition were the Northampton & Banbury Junction Railway (N&BJR) and the East & West Junction Railway (E&WJR), which connected with the LNWR main line at Blisworth. Both were poverty-stricken companies that never achieved their potential. A company promoted by the E&WJR in 1882, and subsequently known as the Stratford-upon-Avon, Towcester & Midland Junction Railway (ST&MJR), opened a line eastwards to join the Midland's branch from Bedford to Northampton at Ravenstone Wood Junction in 1891. This managed to earn some extra revenue by providing a cross-country connection between two main lines of the Midland. In the early twentieth century the companies amalgamated to form the Stratford-upon-Avon & Midland Junction Railway (SMJR).

The last major addition to Northamptonshire's railways was the Great Central Railway (GCR), devised as an extension southwards to London of the Manchester, Sheffield & Lincolnshire Railway (MS&LR), and to be part of a linked system extending via the Channel Tunnel to Paris. It was the last main line to be built and was completed in 1899. Sadly its main promoter, Sir Edward Watkin, one of the last of the heroic figures of the Railway Age was forced to retire through ill health before its completion, and the concept of the international route died with him.

In the Grouping of 1923 the LNWR, Midland and SMJR amalgamated to form the London, Midland & Scottish Railway (LMS); The GNR and GC were merged into the London & North Eastern Railway (LNER), while the GWR remained unaltered so far as Northamptonshire was concerned. The companies were all incorporated into British Railways on nationalisation on 1 January 1948.

At the system's greatest extent Northamptonshire and the Soke possessed 92 passenger stations. Closure of stations began as long ago as 1871 when the N&BJR closed Tiffield Station. The passenger stations on the Towcester to Ravenstone Wood line also had a very short life, from 1 December 1891 to 23 March 1892. The LMS and LNER closed a few stations before the outbreak of war in 1939 and the LMS even closed two during the war, but no lines were closed completely. However, after nationalisation a more systematic closure programme of both lines and stations began. The first to go was the N&BJR which closed completely from Towcester to Cockley Brake Junction in 1951. Following this closures gathered pace, culminating in the Beeching closures after 1963. By 1966 the GCR had gone, along with its connections with the SMJR and the GWR. The final closures were the Northampton to Market Harborough line in 1980 and the rump of the Northampton to Bedford line as far as the MOD depot at Piddington shortly after. Today there are just eight passenger stations open in the whole area covered by this book.

NORTHAMPTONSHIRE'S FIRST MAIN LINE

The London & Birmingham Railway

Passenger service withdrawn	7 September 1964
Distance (in Northants.)	21.4 miles
Companies	L&BR, LNWR, LMS and BR (Midland)

Stations closed	*Date*
Roade	7 September 1964
Blisworth	4 January 1960
Weedon	15 September 1958
Welton	7 July 1958

From the very earliest days of the L&BR there was a station at Roade. The original opened on 17 September 1838 and served as a railhead for Northampton, Kettering, Peterborough and other smaller market towns. The line was soon overloaded with traffic and the original two tracks, nearest the camera, were augmented in 1881 by two more which branched off a mile further north to serve Northampton. The buildings, seen here in April 1959, date from this quadrupling, all except the brick booking office on the far side, which replaced the original during the Second World War, following a fire.

Blisworth Station replaced a temporary wooden one in 1845, following the opening of the LNWR's branch to Northampton and Peterborough. In this photograph, taken fifty years or so later, a down express pauses to make a connection. Its engine is the 3-cylinder compound No. 2053, 'Greater Britain', designed by F.W. Webb and built at Crewe in 1891. The driving wheels of these engines were driven separately by the outside and inside cylinders and thus had the wheel arrangement 2-2-2-2. Tales of the rear driving wheels revolving in a different direction from the front pair would seem to be apocryphal, probably spread by Webb's enemies of which there were more than a few. The photograph underlines the magnificent condition in which the LNWR kept its engines' 'blackberry black' livery. The carriages are painted in the company's celebrated 'plum and spilt milk' colours. The line to Northampton and Peterborough can be seen trailing in the up direction by the second vehicle of the train.

At Weedon the L&BR ran beside the Grand Junction Canal. In the early days it was not envisaged that the railway would handle such a downmarket commodity as coal, but rather that it would leave such bulky and dirty things to the canals and carry light, valuable goods instead. However, it was not long before there was pressure to move coal, which came down the newly opened Midland Counties line to Rugby, from the developing coalfields in Nottinghamshire and Derbyshire. Eventually the L&BR relented and allowed some coal to be taken from Rugby to Weedon at night, in discreetly sheeted wagons. Here it was transhipped from specially built sidings to canal boats for onward forwarding. Transhipment at Weedon went on for many years; local coal merchants who had yards far from the railway were supplied in this method until after the Second World War. The transhipment shed can be seen projecting over the canal. Just beyond the transhipment shed the canal widens and a branch ran from here under the main railway into Weedon Military Depot. A retractable drawbridge, designed by Robert Stephenson, carried the railway over the canal branch at this point.

The original station building at Weedon dated from the opening of the L&BR, but the buildings seen in this photograph, taken on 21 June 1958, three months before closure, date from the construction of the Daventry branch line in 1888. Although the branch was later extended through Braunston to Southam and Leamington, the route was never developed. The view is looking north, with the 2.30 p.m. branch motor (push and pull) train for Leamington waiting for its main line connection, which is signalled on the down line. Small as the station may have appeared, no less than three of Weedon's permanent staff were killed in action during the First World War.

BRANCHES OF THE FIRST MAIN LINE

1. The Leamington branch (Weedon – Daventry – Braunston)

		Stations closed	*Date*
Passenger service withdrawn	15 September 1958	Daventry	15 September 1958
Distance (in Northants.)	7.2 miles	Braunston	15 September 1958
Companies	LNWR, LMS and BR (Midland)		

The canal stronghold of Braunston remained inviolate by railways until 1 August 1895 when the extension from Daventry to Southam and Leamington was opened. Until then the two canal companies, the Oxford and the Grand Junction, had enjoyed a monopoly of traffic in the area. This photograph shows the wooden station building at Braunston, perched high above Braunston Wharf, in its early days. Stations of this size were rarely dignified with the appointment of a stationmaster, but would be in the charge of a Senior Porter who is most probably the watch-chained gentleman standing in the centre of the picture. He would also work the simple lever frame and block telegraph situated in the small building to the right. Another uniformed porter completes the staff; the boy may well have been a general factotum, not yet eligible for uniformed status. Despite its small size, one of Braunston's staff was killed on active service during the First World War.

2. The Nene Valley line (Northampton – Peterborough)

Passenger service withdrawn	4 May 1962
Distance (in Northants.)	41.5 miles
Companies	LNWR, LMS and BR (Midland)

Stations closed	*Date*
Northampton Castle (South bays)	4 May 1964
Northampton (Bridge Street)	4 May 1964
Billing	6 October 1952
Castle Ashby & Earls Barton	4 May 1964
Wellingborough (London Road)	4 May 1964
Ditchford	1 November 1924
Irthlingborough	4 May 1964
Ringstead & Addington	4 May 1964
Thrapston (Bridge Street)	4 May 1964
Thorpe	4 May 1964
Barnwell	4 May 1964
Oundle	4 May 1964
Castor	1 July 1957
Orton Waterville	October 1942
Peterborough East	4 May 1964

The Blisworth line gave Northampton a service to the main line which was independent of loop line trains which went direct to join the main line near Roade from 1881 onwards. Trains for Blisworth, Peterborough and Bedford all started and terminated from platforms at Northampton Castle Station, situated south of West Bridge and shown here, until the final withdrawal of services in 1964. On 5 April 1952 ex-LNWR 2-4-2T engine No. 46666 (LMS 6666), designed in 1890, waits with the Blisworth rail motor in what is now a car park.

Northampton's first railway station was situated where the Peterborough line crossed Bridge Street and opened on 13 May 1845. The station buildings were designed in a sort of Jacobean style which the company doubtless thought reflected Northampton's importance. The line to Market Harborough, opened in 1852, initially joined here in a trailing direction, which prevented direct through running, but a western curve later gave a direct connection from Blisworth, with the town being served by a small station near the castle. After 1881 this became Northampton's main station and Bridge Street's importance declined. Trains nevertheless continued to call until 4 May 1964, when the greater part of the Peterborough line was closed. On 4 July 1959 Class 4F 0-6-0 No. 44578 (ex-LMS 4578) calls with the 12.50 p.m. train from Peterborough to Northampton Castle.

The ultimate downfall of the Northampton to Peterborough line resulted from its many level crossings, all of which were manned. Most of these were adjacent to stations and here we can see an especially complex arrangement at Castle Ashby, where the main line has a crossing operated from the signal box while the goods yard has a separate hand operated arrangement. Photographed on 22 April 1959, an ex-LNER 4-4-0, No. 62613, pulls away with the 12.40 p.m. train for Northampton from Peterborough.

The site of Wellingborough (London Road) Station at Little Irchester has all but vanished beneath a modern flyover on the A45. At one time, however, it marked an important junction between the LNWR line from Northampton to Peterborough and a spur from the Midland main line. From 1857 this gave the Midland access to Northampton where it had its own temporary station near Bridge Street. Wellingborough (London Road) was situated a good mile from the town and this photograph was taken from the top of one of the silos at Victoria Mill, adjoining the station, some time around 1906. This mill had sidings off the Peterborough line as well as unloading gear on the adjacent River Nene to handle its substantial grain traffic. The empty road heading towards the top right leads towards Wollaston and Olney, while the one running from left to right, later the A45, leads from the main London to Carlisle road at Higham Ferrers, later the A6, across the level crossing to Northampton and Wellingborough.

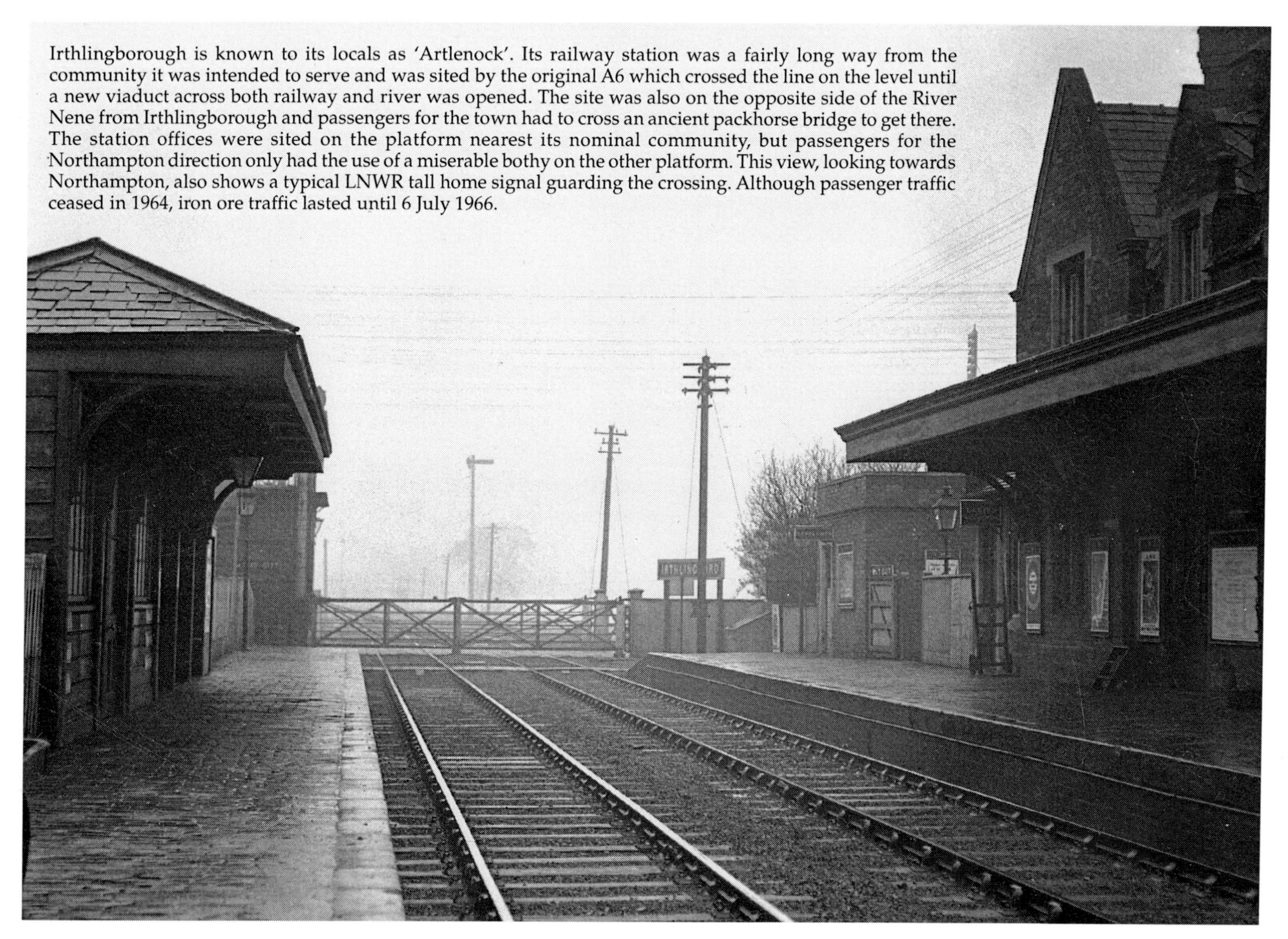

Irthlingborough is known to its locals as 'Artlenock'. Its railway station was a fairly long way from the community it was intended to serve and was sited by the original A6 which crossed the line on the level until a new viaduct across both railway and river was opened. The site was also on the opposite side of the River Nene from Irthlingborough and passengers for the town had to cross an ancient packhorse bridge to get there. The station offices were sited on the platform nearest its nominal community, but passengers for the Northampton direction only had the use of a miserable bothy on the other platform. This view, looking towards Northampton, also shows a typical LNWR tall home signal guarding the crossing. Although passenger traffic ceased in 1964, iron ore traffic lasted until 6 July 1966.

The Peterborough line had some pretty undistinguished looking stations serving the smaller communities and Ringstead & Addington was no exception. The two platforms were staggered and joined by a level crossing, as this photograph, taken from the rear coach of a Northampton-bound train in April 1954 shows. Six years after nationalisation the station still sported its LMS 'Hawkseye' pattern name board and LNWR pattern oil platform lamps.

Thrapston (Bridge Street) was one of the more respectable stations and served a small market town. The level crossing in the foreground carried the main A604 across the line. This photograph was also taken out of the rear of a Northampton-bound train in April 1954. Of interest are the typical LNWR pattern signal box, where the signalman has returned the starting signal to danger behind the train and is already operating the wheel to open the crossing gates, and the locomotive water tank at the far end of the platform. Nothing remains of this scene today.

A large crowd awaits the arrival of a down train at Oundle Station in the early years of the twentieth century. Some of them appear to be Oundle schoolboys, the older ones in boaters and flannels and the younger ones wearing breeches and Eton collars. That the train is a special one seems to be indicated by the somewhat lopsided headboard on the engine's smokebox door. A very typical LNWR locomotive water tank can be seen behind the platform shelter. Although regular passenger traffic ended in May 1964, the station saw some occasional use by special trains for Oundle School for a year after. Freight traffic to Peterborough lasted until 6 June 1972, after which the line was cut back to Yarwell Junction.

Orton Waterville Station was closed by the LMS in 1942, but survived reasonably intact for another twenty years or so. This picture was taken on 7 May 1960 and shows another typical small LNWR signal box and a surviving LNWR lower quadrant stop signal with a corrugated arm. This design of signal was once standard from Euston to Carlisle and was gradually replaced by the LMS standard upper quadrant version, one of which may be seen on the other side of the level crossing. This is one section of line that remains, having been operated by a private preservation company since 1978, although the station and its buildings have been substantially altered.

The end of the line was at Peterborough East, where originally the LNWR made an end-on junction with the Eastern Counties Railway, later the Great Eastern. The Midland also ran into this cramped station and for a while, until its main station was completed, so did the GNR. On 20 May 1938 a Webb 2-4-2T, of 1890 design, stands at the head of a train of two wooden bodied LMS coaches and an ex-LNWR van forming the 6.10 p.m. for Northampton. Note the LNER upper quadrant signal in the foreground.

3. The Bletchley – Banbury line

Passenger service withdrawn	2 January 1961
Distance (in Northants.)	9.5 miles
Companies	LNWR, LMS and BR (Midland)

Stations closed	*Date*
Brackley (London Road)	2 January 1961
Farthinghoe	3 November 1952
Banbury (Merton Street) *	2 January 1961

In this photograph, taken on 15 March 1952, the 3.42 p.m. Midland Region train for Bletchley is about to leave Banbury (Merton Street) behind 2-6-4T No. 42669 (ex-LMS 2669). The connection to Towcester and Blisworth had closed some ten months previously, on 30 June 1951, and goods services had ended the following October. The last passenger train had carried a large Union flag on the engine.

* Used by N&BJR trains until 30 June 1951.

OTHER LINES OF THE LONDON & NORTH WESTERN RAILWAY

1. The Northampton loop

Passenger service withdrawn	13 June 1960
Distance (in Northants.)	17 miles
Companies	LNWR, LMS and BR (Midland)

Stations closed	*Date*
Church Brampton	18 May 1931
Althorp Park	13 June 1960
Long Buckby (first station)	*c.*1964
Kilsby & Crick	1 February 1960

Althorp Park was one of four stations on the 1881 Northampton loop line to Rugby and was built for the convenience of the fourth Earl Spencer, a cabinet minister in W.E. Gladstone's administration. The station often saw British and foreign dignitaries, including the Empress of Austria, who hunted locally with the Pytchley. In spite of the protests of the sixth earl, the station was closed in June 1960 and subsequently demolished.

Although Long Buckby station remains open, it is but a shadow of its old self. When H.C. Casserley took this picture in July 1959 it still had its LNWR canopies to shelter passengers, but Spartan bus-type shelters have since replaced these. Perhaps the station's greatest moment was in September 1997, when the Royal Train arrived here on the occasion of Princess Diana's funeral.

2. The Harborough line (Northampton – Market Harborough)

Passenger service withdrawn	4 January 1960
Distance (in Northants.)	15.9 miles
Companies	LNWR, LMS and BR (Midland)

Stations closed	*Date*
Pitsford & Brampton	5 June 1950
Spratton	23 May 1949
Brixworth	4 January 1960
Lamport	4 January 1960
Kelmarsh	4 January 1960
Clipston & Oxenden	4 January 1960

At the time of writing (early 2003) there is a plan to reopen Lamport Station to serve the preserved Northampton & Lamport Steam Railway. This photograph of the station was taken from a train from Northampton to Market Harborough on 25 June 1955. The LMS station sign surviving seven years after its owners is noteworthy. Although local traffic was sparse, the line from Northampton to Market Harborough survived as a through route. Until 1972 it boasted a Euston to Edinburgh sleeping car express and was closed completely in 1980. Like the slightly earlier Nene Valley line, the Market Harborough line was cheaply built (between 1853 and 1859) with stations a long way from the communities served and many level crossings. These factors contributed to its downfall.

3. The Rugby – Peterborough line

Passenger service withdrawn	6 June 1966
Distance (in Northants.)	18 miles
Companies	LNWR, LMS and BR (Midland)

Stations closed	*Date*
Nassington	6 June 1966
Kingscliffe	6 June 1966
Wakerley & Barrowden	6 June 1966
Ashley & Weston	6 June 1966
Lubenham	6 June 1966
Yelvertoft & Stanford Park	6 June 1966
Lilbourne	6 June 1966

The LNWR was anxious to keep the Midland out of Northamptonshire, and on 1 May 1850 it opened a long, rambling branch from Rugby through Market Harborough towards Stamford and Peterborough. However it never got beyond Luffenham, where it encountered the Midland line from Syston to Peterborough in 1851. In the latter part of the nineteenth century the LNWR underwent a management shake-up and set about improving many of its lines. Amongst these improvements was the opening in 1879 of a new line from Seaton on the old line to Yarwell, near Wansford on the Nene Valley route. This gave the LNWR access to Peterborough and the GER independent of the Midland route through Peterborough North. It had three stations and at one time carried boat trains between Birmingham and Harwich, but eventually fell victim to the Beeching cuts of the 1960s. The picture shows the middle station at Kingscliffe in the early twentieth century.

LINES OF THE MIDLAND RAILWAY

1. The Peterborough – Leicester line

		Stations closed	*Date*
Passenger service withdrawn	Line still open	Walton	6 June 1966
Distance (in Northants.)	10.1 miles	Helpston	6 June 1966
Companies	MR, LMS and BR (Midland)	Uffington & Barnack	1 September 1952

The Midland Railway reached Peterborough in 1846 from Stamford, although politics prevented completion of the route from Luffenham to Syston Junction near Leicester for nearly two years. When the Great Northern line was proposed a deal was made that the GNR would be allowed to run parallel with the Midland between Peterborough and Helpston, provided that the GNR did not build stations at those places. In this view of Helpston Station taken in 1967, after it closed to passengers, the ex-GNR line can just be seen to the right behind the Midland signal box. There were two parallel level crossings, controlled by the two companies independently.

Uffington & Barnack Station closed before the rest of the stations on the Midland line to Leicester, but the station house, of a vernacular cottage style, remained in railway service for a long time after. It is seen here in 1959.

2. The 'Varsity line'

Passenger service withdrawn	15 June 1959
Distance (in Northants.)	13.7 miles
Companies	MR, LMS and BR (Midland)

Stations closed	*Date*
Cranford	2 April 1956
Twywell	30 January 1951
Thrapston (Midland Road)	15 January 1959
Raunds	15 June 1959

A long single tracked branch led from the Midland main line at Kettering to Cambridge and was known by some as the 'Varsity line'. It ran through sparsely populated country in Northamptonshire and Huntingdonshire, but had some trade in ironstone at its northern end. This photograph, which appeared on a postcard posted on 22 March 1907, shows the pretty little station at Cranford. Although this station was closed on 2 April 1956, some three years before the other stations on the line, ironstone traffic from here survived the closure of the rest of the line in June 1959 and lasted until 4 July 1969.

A more important station was Thrapston (Midland Road), seen here in July 1958. Perched high above the western side of the town, the station was another built in the local vernacular style. It perpetuated a somewhat archaic feature, shown here, whereby a barrow crossing was situated opposite the main entrance, resulting in a sudden dip in the main platform. This, and the lowness of the platform itself, were features which would surely not be countenanced today by the Health and Safety Executive. The station represented one of the few passing loops on the line and so had some significance in the timetable. The line never boasted more than four passenger trains each way daily and for much of its latter career there were only three. However, it served its rural communities diligently for ninety-three years, from 1866 until 1959, and gave Thrapston an alternative route to London via the GNR/LNER main line from Huntingdon.

Raunds Station shared with Piddington on the Northampton and Bedford line the prize for remoteness, being some two miles from the village of the same name. The style of the station buildings was very similar to those at Cranford on the same line. A Midland Railway 2-4-0 engine is arriving in this pre-1914 photograph with on of the company's handsome clerestory-roofed carriages.

3. The Kettering – Manton line

Passenger service withdrawn	18 April 1966
Distance (in Northants.)	18 miles
Companies	MR, LMS and BR (Midland)

Stations closed	*Date*
Geddington	1 November 1948
Weldon & Corby	18 April 1966
Gretton	18 April 1966
Harringworth	1 November 1948

The Midland Railway built a cross-country line from Kettering to Manton on its Peterborough to Syston route. Authorised in 1875, the line was completed in 1880 and remains in operation today as a useful relief route between Nottingham and the south, bypassing Leicester. One of its main features is the magnificent Harringworth Viaduct across the Welland Valley. However, although it was very busy with ironstone traffic and served the boom town of Corby, its passenger stations were not the busiest. One of the last to survive was Gretton, seen here in April 1959. Note the typical Midland Railway type of wooden fencing with diagonal slats which, by the time of this photograph, had survived its original owners by 26 years. The station lasted another seven years, closing in 1966 along with Corby.

4. The Northampton – Bedford line

		Stations closed	*Date*
Passenger service withdrawn	5 March 1962	Northampton St Johns	5 July 1939
Distance (in Northants.)	7.1 miles	Piddington	5 March 1962
Companies	MR, LMS and BR (Midland)		

More Midland Railway diagonal slats are in evidence here at Northampton (St Johns), seen some time during the 1930s. This handsome and convenient station was built in the grounds of the mediaeval St Johns Priory and was some three minutes walk from Northampton Market Place. It was opened in 1872 and served the Bedford and Wellingborough lines, the latter by running powers over the LNWR's Nene Valley line. At one time a series of fast services to Wellingborough and Kettering with connections for Leicester ran from this station, with as many as 12 trains a day in 1901.

The LMS had three stations in Northampton after 1923 and it was evident that this was a luxury that the company could ill afford. Accordingly St Johns was closed in 1939. Latterly, services were worked by locomotives 'cascaded' from more important duties, and here, pictured at St Johns in 1930, ex-LNWR No. 5031, 'Hardwicke', once the star of the famous 'Race to the North' of 1896, is relegated to hauling the 2.18 p.m. train from St Johns to Wellingborough. Happily 'Hardwicke' is preserved and may be viewed in the National Railway Museum at York. The wooden construction in the background is a cooling tower at Northampton Corporation's Bridge Street Power Station, which supplied power for the corporation's electric trams.

5. The Higham Ferrers branch

Passenger service withdrawn	15 June 1959	*Stations closed*	*Date*
Distance (in Northants.)	5 miles	Higham Ferrers	15 June 1959
Companies	MR, LMS and BR (Midland)	Rushden	15 June 1959

The Midland's branch line from Wellingborough to Higham Ferrers opened at the comparatively late date of 1 May 1894. It was intended to continue the line to join with the 'Varsity' line near Raunds, but opposition from a local landowner prevented this so the line remained a dead end. At one time a somewhat makeshift push-and-pull unit operated the passenger service, the passengers being accommodated in a downgraded Pullman car with the control rods rattling overhead through the clerestory roof. The line had been open for about ten years when this photograph was taken, showing a train entering Rushden Station bunker first with a train for Wellingborough. Note the formation left wide enough for doubling the track at some future date and the thoughtfully placed smoke shield on the footbridge above the vacant trackbed. Although the line closed to passengers in 1959 and to goods on 1 September 1969, the station has survived and has been preserved for future generations to experience what a Midland Railway country branch station was like.

6. The Midland main line

Passenger service withdrawn	7 March 1960	*Stations closed*	*Date*
Distance (in Northants.)	20.5 miles	Desborough & Rothwell	1 January 1968
Companies	MR, LMS and BR (Midland)	Glendon & Rushton	4 January 1960
		Isham & Burton Latimer	4 January 1960
		Finedon	December 1940
		Irchester	7 March 1960

The Midland Railway's first incursion into Northamptonshire was the Leicester to Hitchen (Herts.) line, begun in June 1853 and opened throughout in May 1857. Eventually the company built its own line to London from Bedford to St Pancras, which opened in 1868, but the section of the line north of Glendon Junction, near Kettering, remained in more or less its original condition for the next century. This photograph of Desborough & Rothwell Station, taken on 10 June 1960, shows a number of individual Midland features, including the station nameboard (albeit with BR-style lettering) inclined slightly to face arriving passengers, diagonally slatted fencing, a distinctive footbridge and goods shed, massive telegraph posts and standard station buildings. It was typical of many smaller wayside stations all over the Midland system, which by 1922 stretched from Southend to Swansea via Derby and from Carlisle to Bath. The runner beans set in the stationmaster's garden behind the up platform shelter are also typical!

THE GREAT NORTHERN RAILWAY AND ITS ASSOCIATED LINE

1. The Great Northern Railway

Passenger service withdrawn	17 June 1963
Distance	8.6 miles
Companies	GNR, M&GNJR, LNER and BR (Eastern)

Stations closed	*Date*
Peakirk	17 June 1963
Barnack	1 July 1929
Ufford Bridge	1 July 1929
Wansford Road	1 July 1929

Although Peterborough (North) is still open (now merely called Peterborough), the old GNR overall roof was demolished when the station was rebuilt in the 1970s. The old station, seen here, dated from the opening of the route from London Kings Cross to Doncaster on 7 August 1850, and by the mid-twentieth century had become a serious bottleneck. This view, taken in 1938 during LNER days, shows the old station with a down semi-fast from Kings Cross headed by ex-GNR 4-4-0 No. 1050.

This picture of Barnack GNR station shows a particularly tall example of the company's distinctive 'somersault' type signal. The company adopted this device following a bad accident in 1876, involving the Flying Scotsman express, at Abbots Ripton, south of Peterborough, when it was found that the primary cause was the then common slotted post semaphore signals becoming clogged with driven snow and showing a false 'clear' indication. With the new type the arm was held separate from the post and dropped at a steep angle to indicate 'all clear'. The Marquis of Exeter of nearby Burghley House promoted this line from Stamford to Wansford in 1867. He had already paid for a branch from the main GNR to Stamford earlier that year. Both lines were worked by the GNR which later took a long lease. Like the other GNR line to Stamford, this was intended to break the Midland's monopoly over the town, towards which the Marquis's family had a proprietorial interest. The GNR trains ran into a bay at Wansford Station on the LNWR's Northampton and Peterborough line, thus giving Stamford people an alternative route to the Midlands, although a dispute with the LNWR caused the junction at Wansford to be severed for nine years until 1878. The line soon succumbed to motor competition and was closed by the LNER in 1929.

2. The Midland & Great Northern Joint Railway

Passenger service withdrawn	2 December 1957	*Stations closed*	*Date*
Distance	10.2 miles	Eye Green	2 December 1957
Companies	GNR, M&GNJR, LNER and BR (Eastern)	Thorney	2 December 1957

Yet another railway company entering Peterborough was the Midland & Great Northern Joint Railway (M&GNJR), taken over from earlier ailing companies by the two larger concerns in 1888. The line gave the Midland and GNR access to the North Norfolk Coast and Lowestoft and Yarmouth. It remained an independent line, with characteristics of both companies, until nationalisation. It was finally closed to all traffic in 1957. This photograph, which appeared on a postcard sent in 1910, shows the large brickworks, which the line both promoted and served at Eye Green, one of two stations in the Soke. Today, a few industrial buildings still occupy the brickworks site, but the line has vanished completely under the A47 Eye bypass.

RAILWAYS OF WEST NORTHAMPTONSHIRE

1. The Great Western Railway

Passenger service withdrawn	2 November 1964	*Stations closed*	*Date*
Distance (in Northants.)	7 miles	Aynho	2 November 1965
Companies GWR, GCR, LNER, BR (Eastern); E&WJR, N&BJR, ST&MJR, SMJR, LMS and BR (Midland).		Aynho Park Platform	7 January 1963

The GWR is not often associated with Northamptonshire, but it did in fact enter the very south western tip of the county. Nevertheless, its presence forced the formation of the LNWR in 1846 and affected both the prosperity and development of the GCR and the SMJR. The first line was a single broad gauge extension northwards from Oxford to Banbury, reached in 1850. This line was doubled when the line was extended to Birmingham two years later. Kings Sutton Station, seen here in March 1955, once again underlines the different character of each railway company. The spear-topped iron fencing and vertical palings could be found from Northamptonshire to Cornwall, as could the GWR pattern gas lamps and the bold Roman typeface used for the nameboard. Although the station is one of the few remaining open in Northamptonshire, it lost its stone buildings and verandah awning in favour of an anonymous bus-type shelter after the staff were withdrawn on 2 November 1964.

A fine view of Aynho Station in June 1939, with a southbound coal train hauled by one of the GWR's impressive 2-8-0 goods engines, No. 2875. The width between the platforms indicates that this was once a broad gauge line. Northamptonshire's last broad gauge trains ran in 1869. It was at this station that a humiliating accident befell the first special train to Birmingham on the broad gauge on 1 October 1852. The directors' special train, headed by the prestigious engine 'Lord of the Isles' – on the footplate of which, in addition to the driver and fireman, were no less exalted persons than Isambard Kingdom Brunel, originator of the broad gauge, and Daniel Gooch, the Chief Mechanical Engineer of the GWR – ran into the local pick-up goods train. The footplate crew had misread a disused signal and 'Lord of the Isles' hit the back of the departing local at speed. The width of the broad gauge saved the day and the special remained upright, although 'Lord of the Isles', which had been displayed the year before at the Great Exhibition, was sorely dented. Nobody was killed, but a few suffered cuts and bruises. The special eventually reached Leamington hauled by the engine of the local train. In the distance can be seen the flyover which carries the cut-off line from Princes Risborough which opened in 1909. Otherwise, in this photograph from June 1939, the station looks much the same as it would have done on its opening day, eighty years previously. It was closed, along with other stations between Banbury and Oxford, in 1965. Some of the stone buildings seen here still survive.

2. The Great Central Railway

Passenger service withdrawn 3 September 1966
Distance (in Northants.) 18 miles
Companies GWR, GCR, LNER, BR (Eastern); E&WJR, N&BJR, ST&MJR, SMJR, LMS and BR (Midland).

Stations closed	*Date*
Cherwelton	4 March 1963
Woodford & Hinton	3 September 1966
Culworth	29 September 1958
Helmdon	4 March 1963
Brackley Central	3 September 1966

Cynics said of the GCR's predecessor, the MS&LR that its initials stood for 'Money Sunk and Lost'. After the change of name the same cynics said that the initials stood for 'Gone Completely'. This view of Cherwelton Station, taken on 27 July 1946, in LNER days, would appear to bear this harsh judgement out. But, in fact, the line through Northamptonshire saw very heavy traffic at times, especially during the two world wars. The GCR was laid out for high speed running for the proposed expresses from Manchester (Central) to Paris (Nord) and this picture illustrates the distinctive GCR layout of an island platform for the slow lines with what would have been the fast lines passing on the outside, well clear of the platforms. In this case though, the outer lines were merely used as goods relief lines, hence the facing points into the goods yard by the upper quadrant starter signal. Such an arrangement would have been forbidden had the lines been through running ones.

The GCR's most important station in Northamptonshire was at Woodford & Hinton, seen here looking north, *c.*1910. The island platform layout has been added to by a wooden platform on the left, used by trains from the SMJR at Byfield. Woodford followed the standard GCR practice of siting stations by over or under bridges. In this case entrance was from below, with passengers climbing a flight of stairs from the road.

An SMJR engine waiting in the up platform at Woodford & Hinton with a GCR coach. The engine is 2-4-0 No. 6, built by Beyer, Peacock & Co. of Manchester in 1884 and obtained by the SMJR's predecessors second-hand the following year. It was withdrawn from service in August 1916. Some trains ran merely to Byfield, some through to Stratford-upon-Avon, while some worked through carriages from the GCR's London terminus at Marylebone to Stratford, which were detached from down trains at Woodford (later known as Woodford Halse). The coach appears to be in varnished teak livery, which dates the picture from after 1910.

A line-up of GCR engines outside the running shed at Woodford & Hinton in the early 1900s. The village's population rose from 527 in the 1891 census to 1,220 by 1901, of whom about 550 were in railway service. The company built 136 staff houses in the village to house the small army of employees needed to service this important junction. The engine running shed had six parallel roads to accommodate engines under cover for maintenance work. The three engines on the left are goods 0-6-0s, while 4-4-0 express engine No. 565, designed by Harry Pollitt for the MS&LR, is on the right.

Brackley Station looking north in June 1958. In this case the station offices were at the top of the cutting side on the left, with passengers reaching the trains by means of the footbridge across the down line. The office buildings survive, as do the fir trees planted by the GCR. In 1923 the GCR became part of the LNER, but retained much of its character, although certain standardised features gradually appeared. After nationalisation in 1947 it became part of the Eastern Region of British Railways, but was transferred to the Midland Region on 1 February 1958. From that time on it was gradually run down in favour of the other Midland Region north to south lines. Expresses were withdrawn in 1960 and the line was closed to freight traffic on 5 April 1965 and to passengers on 3 September 1966. The whole length of the line in Northamptonshire has been lifted and most of the bridges and viaducts demolished. A plan is now current to relay the line from London to Rugby in order to relieve the motorways of freight traffic to and from Euro tunnel.

3. The Banbury branch (Great Central Railway)

Passenger service withdrawn	2 April 1966
Distance (in Northants.)	9.5 miles
Companies	GWR, GCR, LNER, BR (Eastern); E&WJR, N&BJR, ST&MJR, SMJR, LMS and BR (Midland).

Stations closed	*Date*
Eydon road Platform	2 April 1956
Chacombe Road Platform	6 February 1956

A short but vital link connected the main GCR near Culworth with the GWR at Banbury. This gave the GWR a most useful connection with the North East, with through carriages running as far as Edinburgh and Aberdeen, and giving direct connection from Nottingham and Leicester with the south coast and channel ports. Very heavy freight traffic also developed, which during wartime was almost continuous. There were two small halts on this line serving Eydon and Chalcombe. This picture shows the standard GCR signal box and wooden platform perched on an embankment at Chalcombe Road on 5 April 1954.

4. The Stratford-upon-Avon & Midland Junction Railway

Passenger service withdrawn	7 April 1952
Distance (in Northants.)	17.4 miles
Companies	GWR, GCR, LNER, BR (Eastern); E&WJR, N&BJR, ST&MJR, SMJR, LMS and BR (Midland).

Stations closed	*Date*
Blisworth	5 April 1952
Tiffield	1 March 1871
Towcester	7 April 1952
Blakesley	7 April 1952
Morton Pinkney	7 April 1952
Byfield	5 April 1952

Although it had a complex and poverty-stricken history, the SMJR had a certain dash and panache, exemplified in this picture of a train for Stratford-upon-Avon leaving Blisworth SMJR station. The cleanliness of the engine and the tidiness of the track are apparent. The engine is the nearest that the company had to an express engine and is 2-4-0 No. 13, built by Beyer, Peacock of Manchester in 1903. The little company styled itself 'The Shakespeare Route' and struggled manfully to provide a competitive service from the LNWR at Blisworth, where its station adjoined the bigger company, connected by a subway. The trucks in the background are on the exchange sidings between the LNWR main line and the SMJR line. Although the N&BJR had running powers over the LNWR line from Blisworth to Northampton (Bridge Street) these were never exercised, one reason being the complex movements required to get N&BJR trains across the LNWR main line. The layout also prevented trains running directly from one company to another. Even in LMS days the two systems remained largely separate, although at various times attempts were made to run through coaches.

When the SMJR was formed out of several near-bankrupt companies in 1908, it carried out a thorough remodelling of Towcester Station, which is seen here in its original condition in this postcard photograph which was posted in Towcester in 1906. Towcester was in many ways the most important station on the SMJR after Stratford-upon-Avon. It was a railway crossroads, albeit of not very important lines! The camera is facing towards Banbury and Stratford and a down train is evidently expected by the porter waiting on the otherwise deserted down platform. According to the inscription on the rear of the postcard, this man's name was John Humphrey, while one of the group opposite was Billy Conron. The cluster of milk churns by the station nameboard on the right is a reminder that the railways performed a vital service to agriculture. At a time of falling cereal and stock prices, the movement of milk and dairy products to the growing towns was one way in which farmers could still make a reasonable living.

A later view of Blakesley Station than the one on the front cover, showing the Blakesley Hall Railway platform right by the base of the down starter signal. By this time a fence had replaced the hedge seen in the other picture.

The E&WJR station at Byfield was opened to passengers on 1 June 1871, but during a black period in the company's finances services were suspended between 31 July 1877 until 22 March 1885. After the opening of the GCR in 1898, Byfield became the most important of the line's village stations because it became an interchange. This photograph dating from E&WJR times, probably taken in the summer of 1906, shows a large locomotive water tank by the overbridge – Byfield was the only place in the 33½ miles between Stratford and Towcester where locomotive water was available. Latterly, this tank was filled with a steam pump, but in earlier times a donkey harnessed to a pole supplied power. The station staff would sometimes increase output by commandeering a horse from a field beside the line during hours of darkness. The steam engine also drove a generator, which made Byfield Station the first SMJR installation to be lit by electricity. A thrifty company arranged for the signalman to spend half his time as signalman and half as pump attendant. The E&WJR was lightly laid, using flat-bottomed rail. The down line is laid with bullhead rail. One of the first acts of the new company in 1908 was to relay a considerable amount of E&WJR track, which improved both the appearance of the permanent way and the riding of the rolling stock.